Guess What

Published in the United States of America by
Cherry Lake Publishing
Ann Arbor, Michigan
www.cherrylakepublishing.com

Content Adviser: Susan Heinrichs Gray
Reading Adviser: Marla Conn MS, Ed., Literacy specialist, Read-Ability, Inc.
Book Designer: Felicia Macheske

Library of Congress Cataloging-in-Publication Data

Names: Macheske, Felicia, author.
Title: Round and rare—giant panda / Felicia Macheske.
Description: Ann Arbor : Cherry Lake, 2017. | Series: Guess what | Includes
 index. | Audience: Grades K to 3.
Identifiers: LCCN 2016029428| ISBN 9781634721707 (hardcover) | ISBN
 9781634722360 (pdf) | ISBN 9781634723022 (pbk.) | ISBN 9781634723688 (ebook)
Subjects: LCSH: Giant panda—Juvenile literature.
Classification: LCC QL737.C27 M224 2017 | DDC 599.789—dc23
LC record available at https://lccn.loc.gov/2016029428

Cherry Lake Publishing would like to acknowledge the work of The Partnership for 21st Century Skills.
Please visit *www.p21.org* for more information.

Printed in the United States of America
Corporate Graphics

Table of Contents

I have patches on my eyes.

I have thick **fur** to keep me warm.

I am very shy.

My favorite food is bamboo.

I like to eat and rest and eat and rest.

My special paWS help me to hold my food.

I was very small when I was born.

I am **playful** and I like to **climb** trees.

Do you know what I am?

I'm a Giant Panda!

About Giant Pandas

1. Giant pandas weigh about 3 to 5 ounces (85 to 142 grams) when they are born. They grow to more than 200 pounds (91 kilograms) as adults.

2. Giant pandas have a large wrist bone that sticks out. It is used like a thumb to hold bamboo.

3. Though they eat mostly bamboo, giant pandas sometimes eat small animals.

4. Giant pandas are **rare**. There are about 1,000 to 2,000 in the **wild**.

5. Wild giant pandas live in China in thick mountain forests.

Glossary

bamboo (bam-BOO) a plant with a hollow, woody stem

patches (PACH-iz) small areas of black fur

rare (RAIR) not often seen or found

wild (WILDE) an area that has been left in its natural state

Index